Drawing Amazing Doodle Dogs

Learning to Draw ZenDoodle Dogs FAST and EASY!

by Veronica Kim

Drawing Amazing Doodle Dogs

Learning to Draw ZenDoodle Dogs FAST and EASY!

by Veronica Kim

Introduction

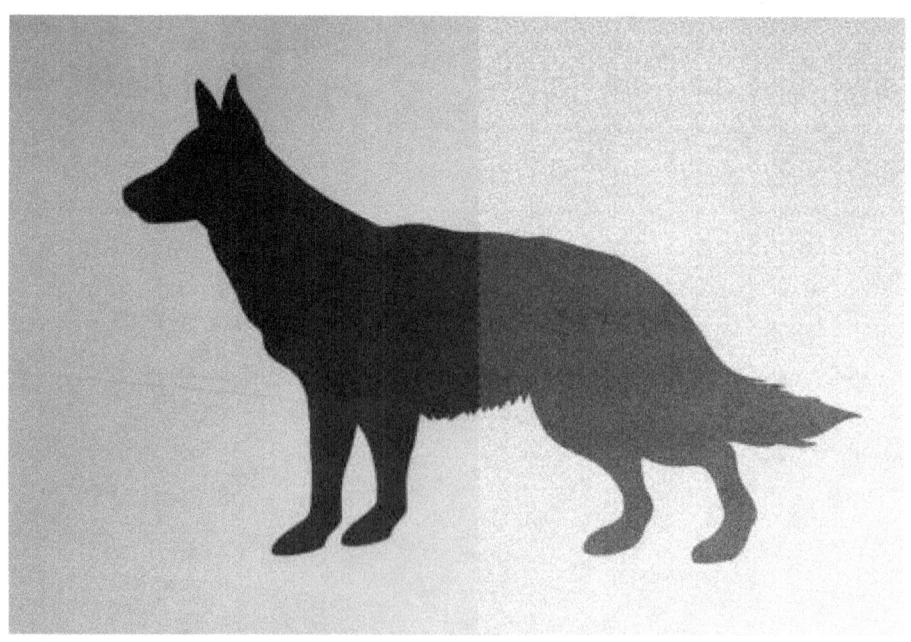

Conclusion

Disclaimer

While all attempts have been made to verify the information provided in this book, the author does assume any responsibility for errors, omissions, or contrary interpretations of the subject matter contained within. **The information provided in this book is for educational and entertainment purposes only. The reader is responsible for his or her own actions and the author does not accept any responsibilities for any liabilities or damages, real or perceived, resulting from the use of this information.**

The trademarks that are used are without any consent, and the publication of the trademark is without permission or backing by the trademark owner. All trademarks and brands within this book are for clarifying purposes only and are the owned by the owners themselves, not affiliated with this document.

Introduction

Dogs are such adorable animals and it is there to a great degree well disposed nature combined with exceptional faithfulness that makes these creatures a most loved family unit pet. Knowing how to draw a puppy isn't that enormous a test truly; it includes fundamental strides to kick us off and after some time these strides can be enhanced to make it quite a lot more reasonable.

Step One: Orienting Oneself with the Features

Take a photo of a pooch face front and portrayal a vertical line to separate the puppy's face into equal parts, a vertical line that cuts over the eyes, two vertical lines to speak to the top and base of the nose, and a vertical line each to speak to the highest point of his head and his mouth. Figuring out how to draw a puppy starts with this fundamental outline so we know where to put the eyes, nose and mouth. This will likewise assist us with verifying that the canine's components are consummately adjusted.

Step Two: Draw a Rough Sketch

Since we have the essential layout as the preparatory stride in knowing how to draw a puppy, we will now utilize bended lines that are daintily drawn to speak to the creature's eyes, gag, ears, nose and hide. The dogs eyes are drawn in circles with the iris shaded in and utilization bended lines to layout the gag's state. Draw two lines from the highest point of the half circle piece of the gag down to the nose, and gently outline the ears. Note the adjustments in shading and plane and imprint particular limits particularly around the eyes.

Step Three: Look Beyond the Outline

The third stride in figuring out how to draw a puppy obliges us to look past the framework and to outline the knocks and hide. Begin drawing the body and if one's photograph of a canine is that of the creature taking a seat, begin outlining the state of his body. The way to making it a sensible drawing is to look carefully, think and draw the lines with most extreme certainty.

Step Four: Indicate the Shadows and Fill in the Colors

In figuring out how to draw particularly how to draw a pooch, there's dependably the component of lighting. In the event that the light is originating from the upper right, one ought to verify that the creature's piece on the base left ought to be hued in a darker tone. It's a smart thought to place accentuation on the puppy's eyes and shade in shadows.

Chapter 1 – How to draw and sketch a dog

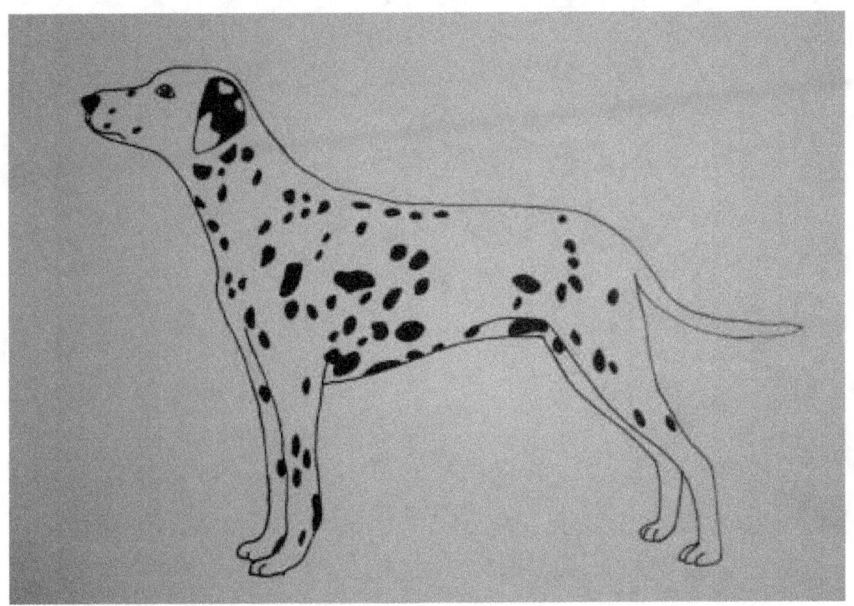

Step 1: Draw two ovals. They ought to be one next to the other. Make one somewhat bigger than the other. Verify they're not very far separated. That is key in this drawing.

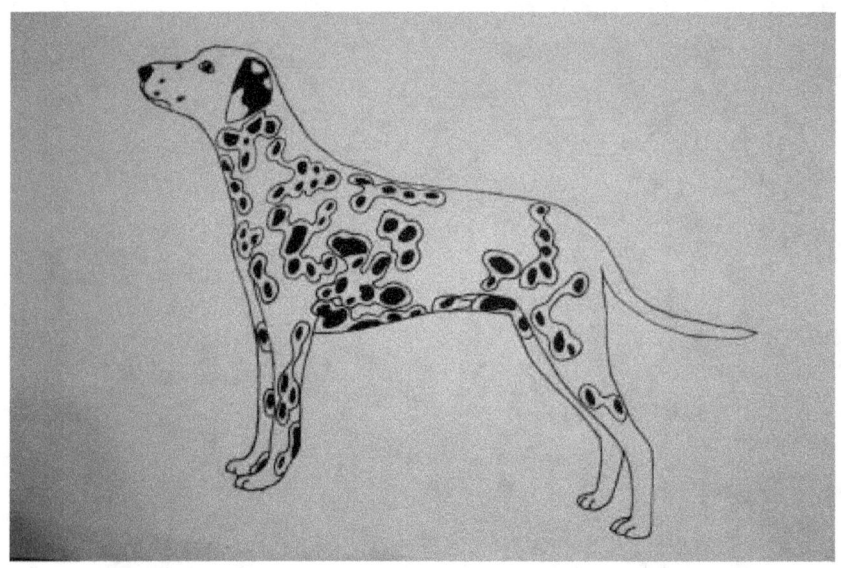

Step 2: Make a framework. Draw a line that goes down and goes on top of the ovals you've made. At that point draw one under it doing likewise. On the last one, curve in a little in the middle of ovals. At that point draw the beginnings of legs, as attracted the photo. Make the base and top lines go up, then

draw a circle for the start of a head. Draw a nose by drawing an oval that is in part in the head.

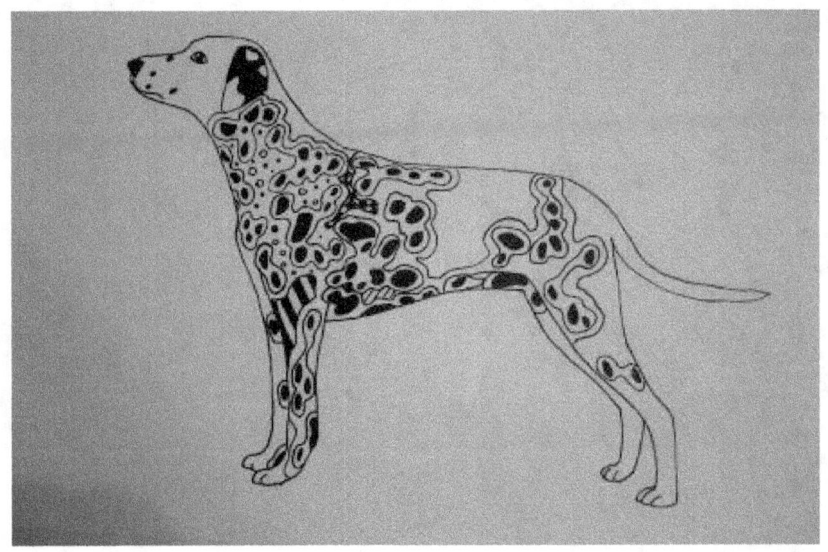

Step 3: Draw lines sketching out the head. Do likewise to the head as you did to the body. After this, delete the circles in the body and head. Add ears to the head that are either long and floppy, or short and up. At that point include either a short or long tail. Right now, it's great to have a chosen breed personality a primary concern, as this it where every one of the subtle elements seem to be.

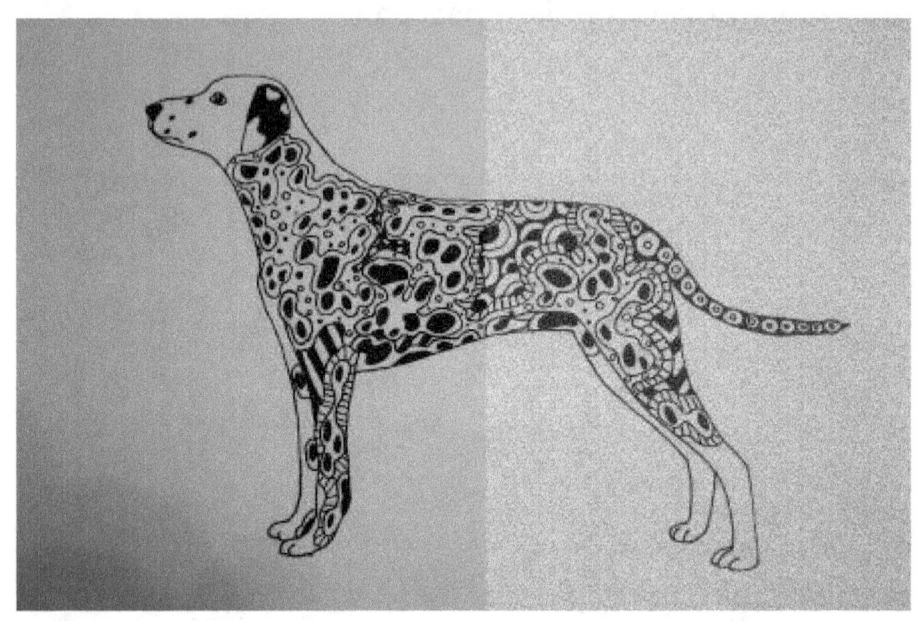

Step 4: Erase every single inward circle. Precisely eradicate the majority of your circles and ovals. At that point include hide by drawing unsettles the layouts. Your dog ought to be extremely sensible!

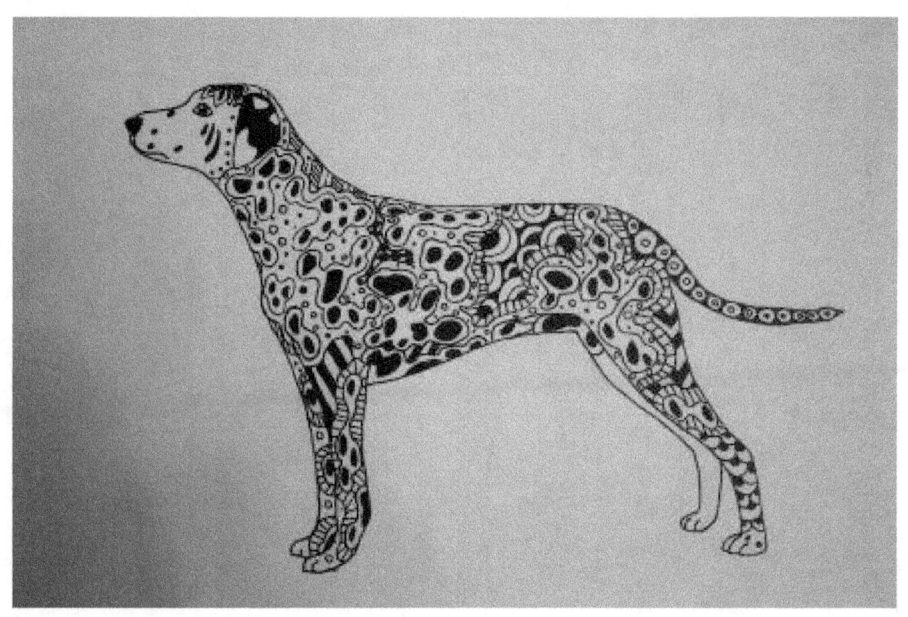

Step 5: Finished. Also, now you can chip away at the shading piece of the dog, since that is the thing that matters a great deal in this picture.

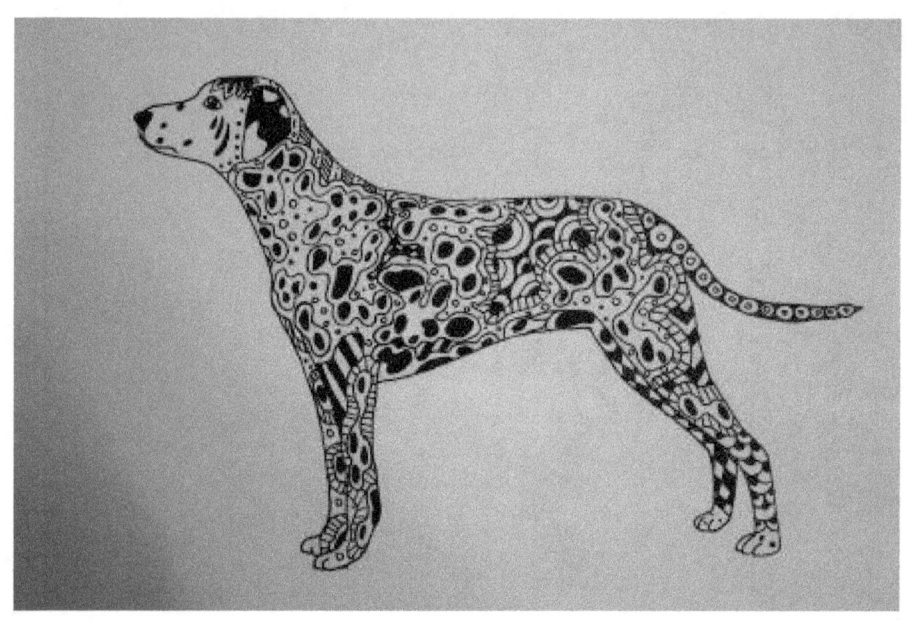

Step 6: Now we have come up with the final image for our sketch of this 1st figure. We have mainly concentrated on the sketching in this figure as you can see.

Chapter 2 – Image 2

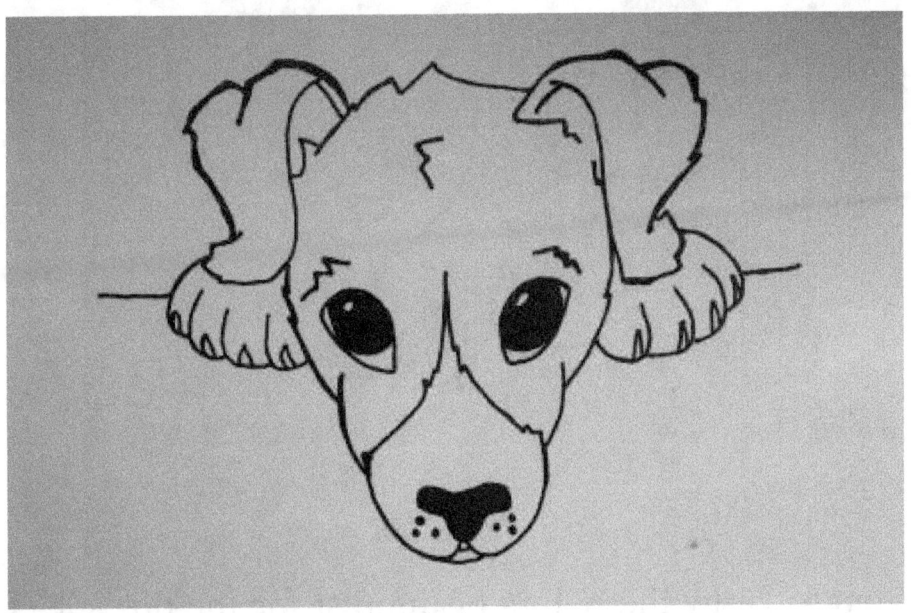

Step 1: Draw two circles of distinctive sizes and an oval for the system.

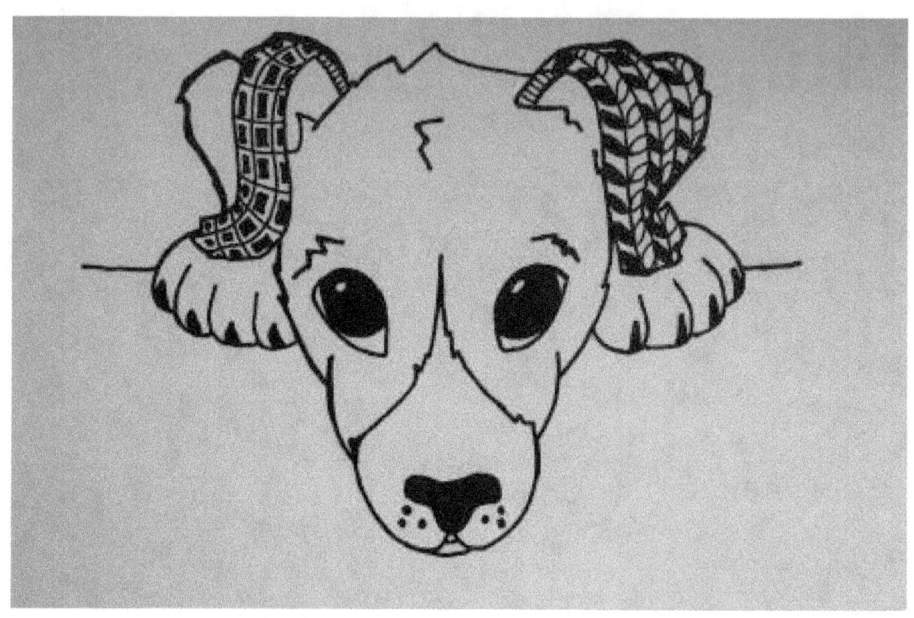

Step 2: Draw the points of interest for the dog's legs utilizing straight lines. Draw utilizing basic shapes as trapezoids, rectangles, and polygons.

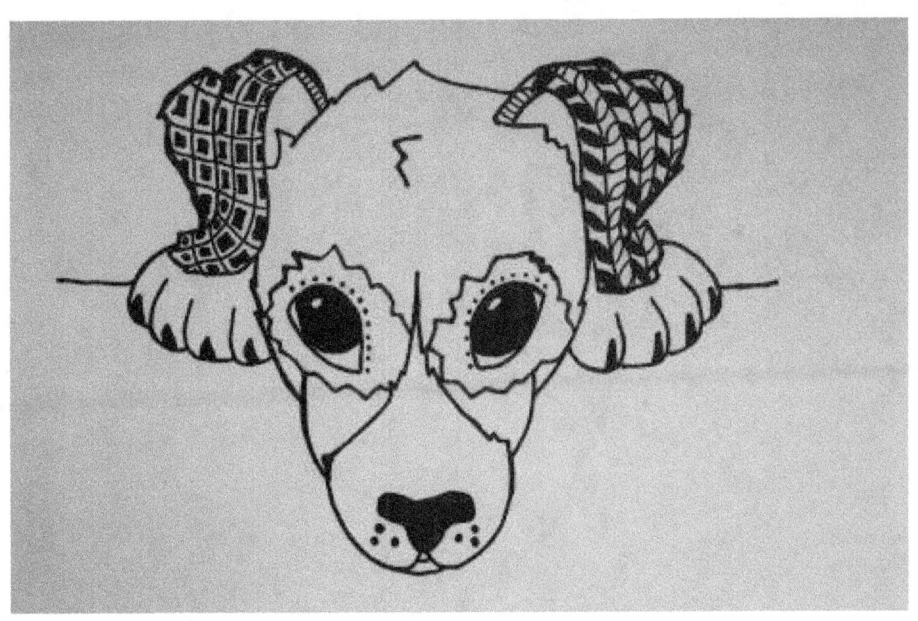

Step 3: Draw the dog's body utilizing bend lines joining the circles and oval.

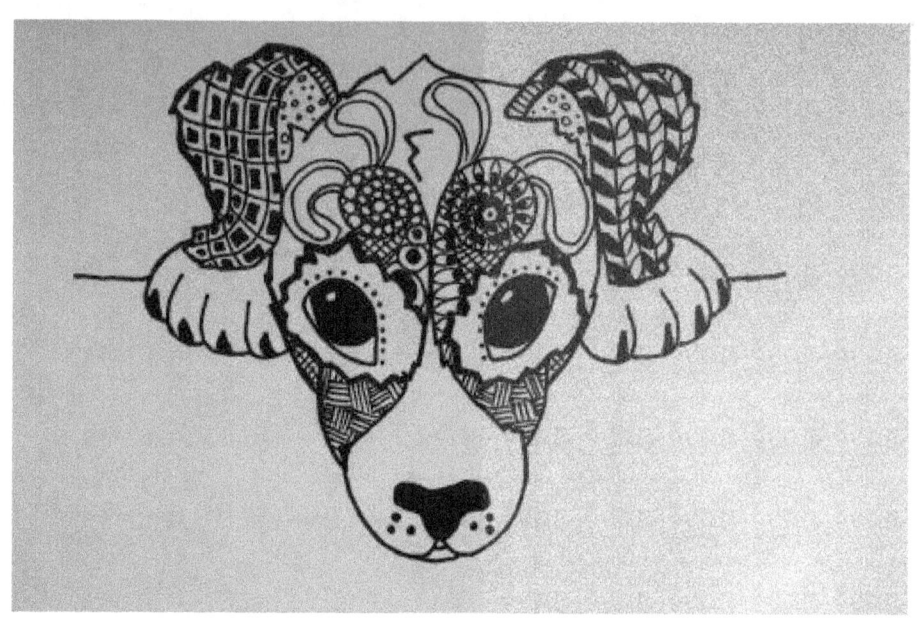

Step 4: Draw points of interest of the dog's head utilizing bend lines. Refine the attracting to make unmistakable the dog's eyes, ears, nose, nose, and mouth.

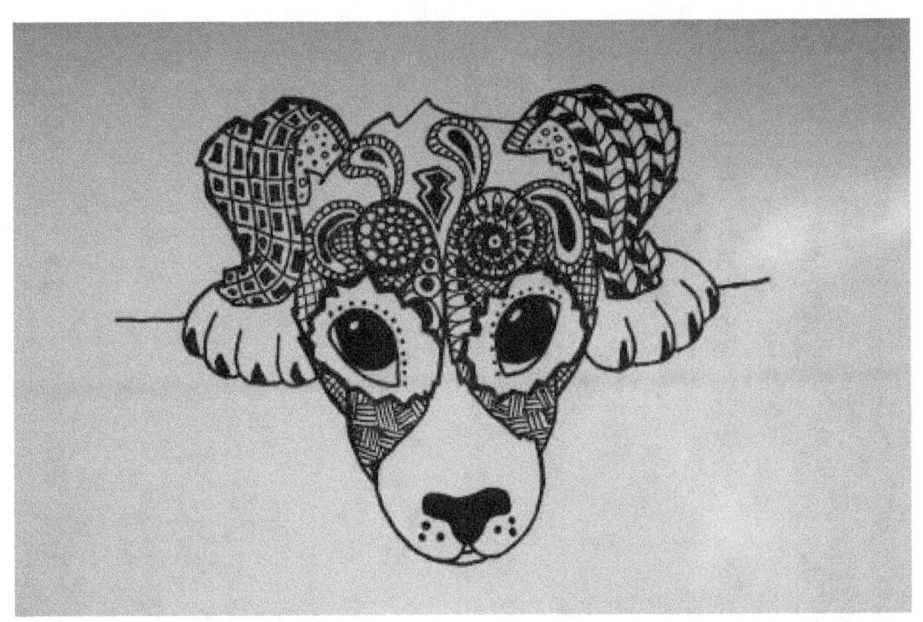

Step 5: Trace with a pen and delete pointless lines.

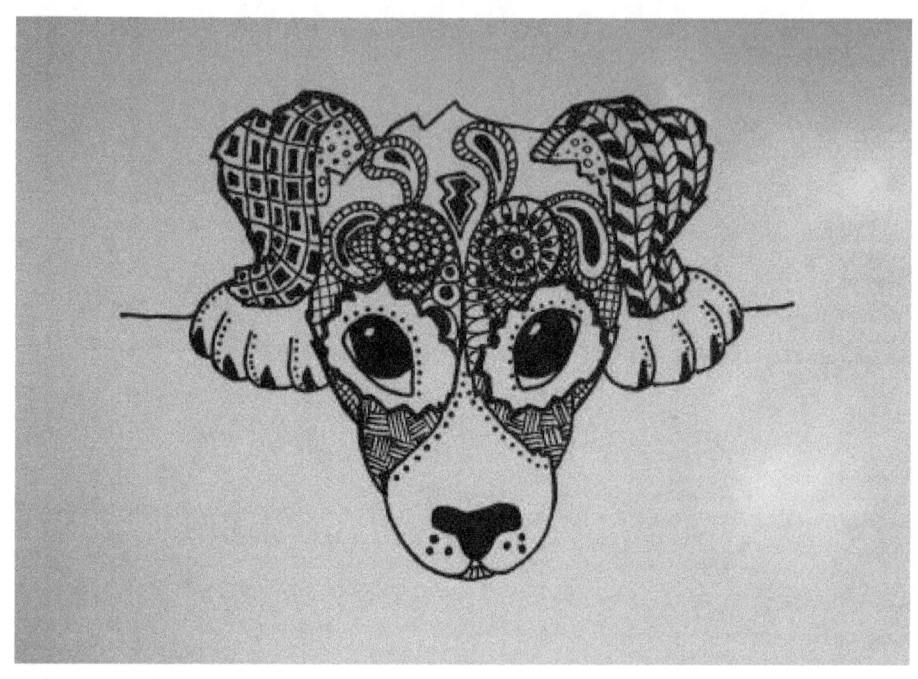

Step 6: Color or portrayal as indicated by you're enjoying!

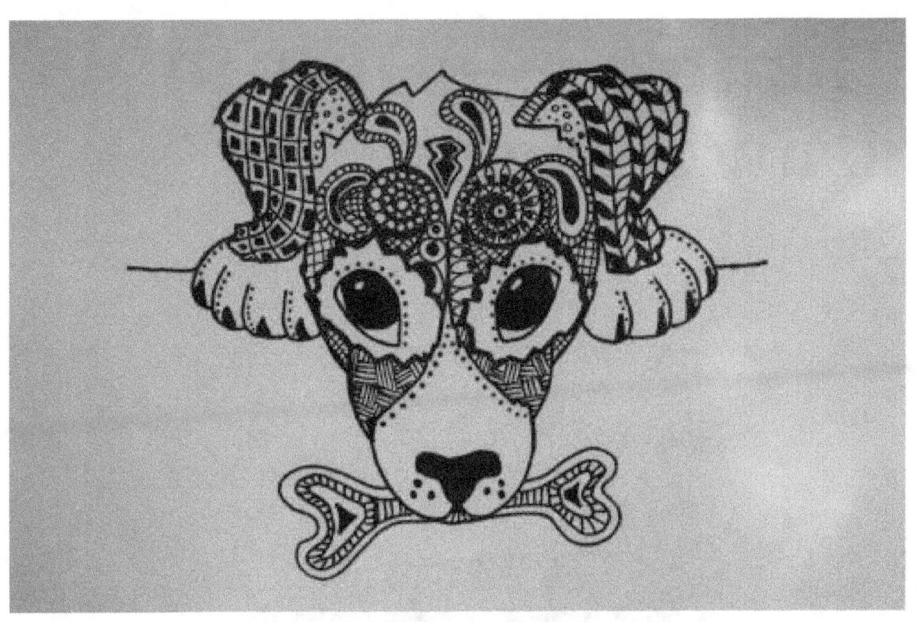

Step 7: Now we have completed the final image of the dog with the bone and with the help of fine sketching.

Chapter 3 – How to draw image 3

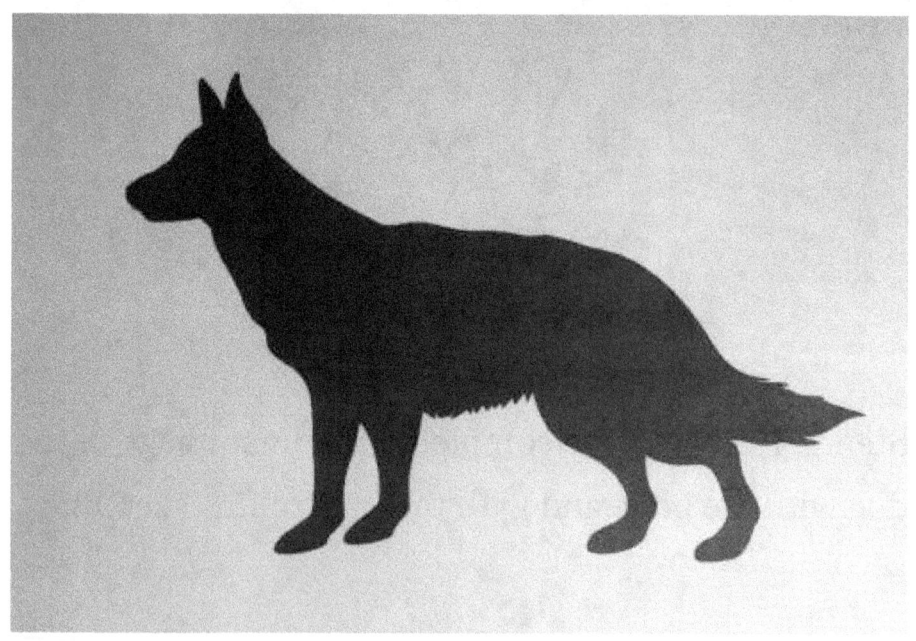

Step 1: Draw not doing so great of your puppy.

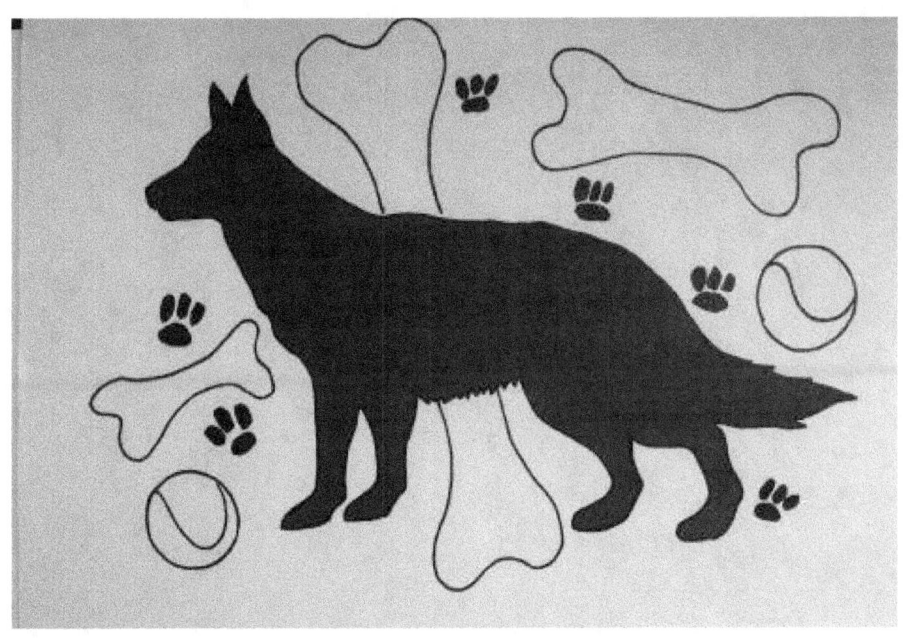

Step 2: Draw in the network for eyes, nose and mouth position.

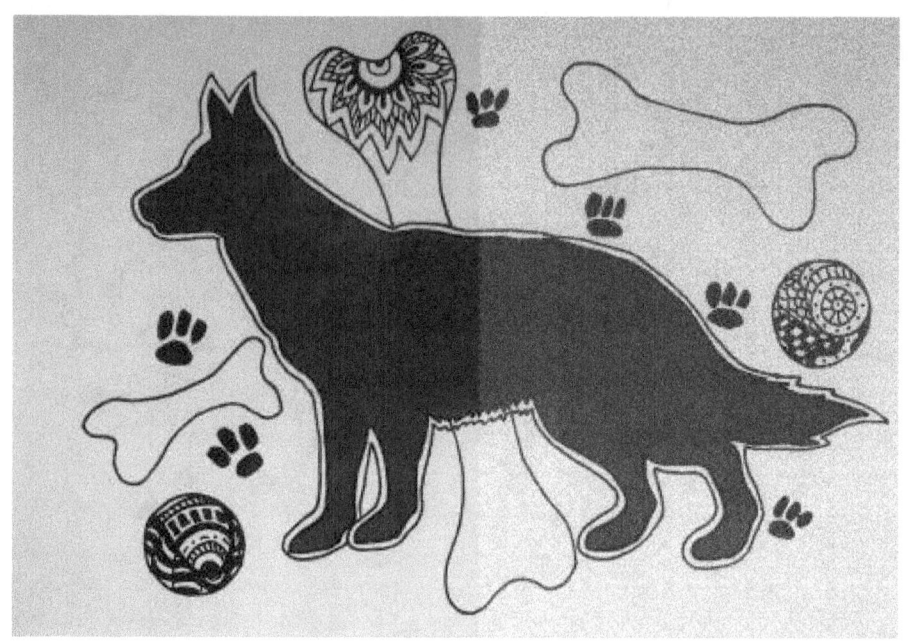

Step 3: Now generally attract the eyes, nose and mouth into the network.

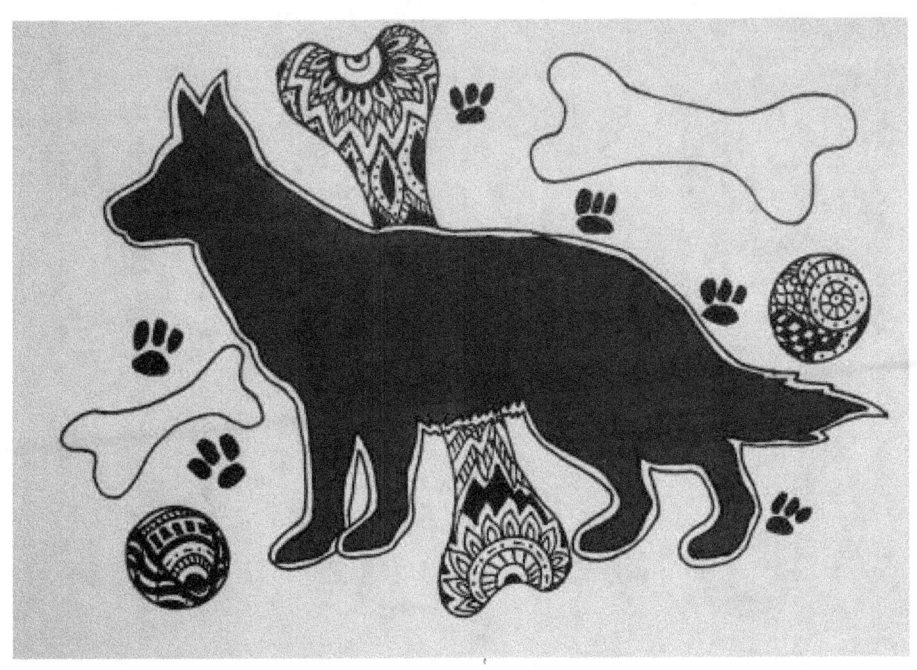

Step 4: With another sheet of paper covering your network, attract the eyes, nose and mouth.

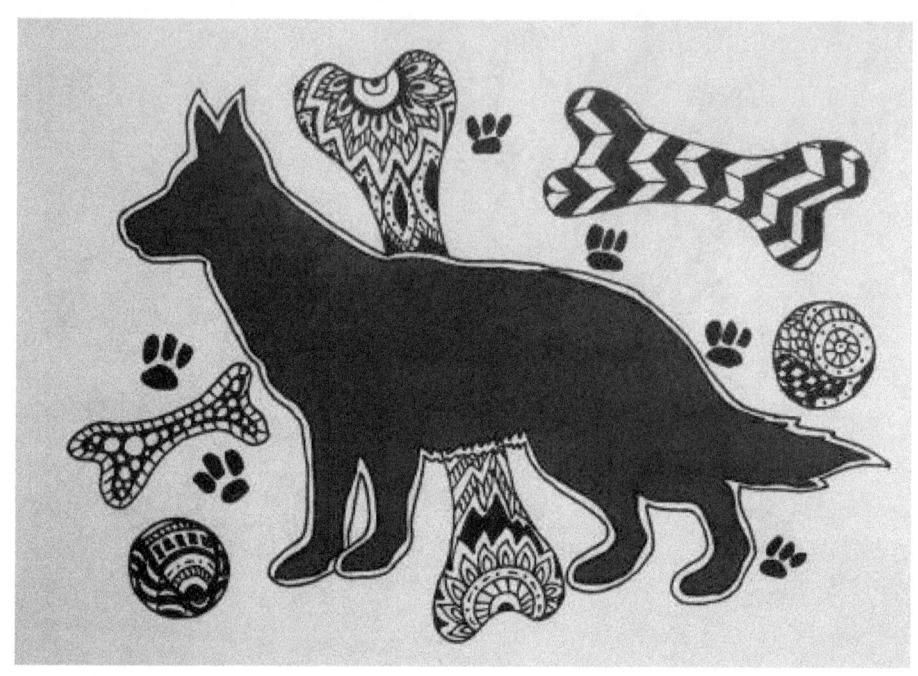

Step 5: Now begin attracting the hide around left ear. Study the picture for direction.

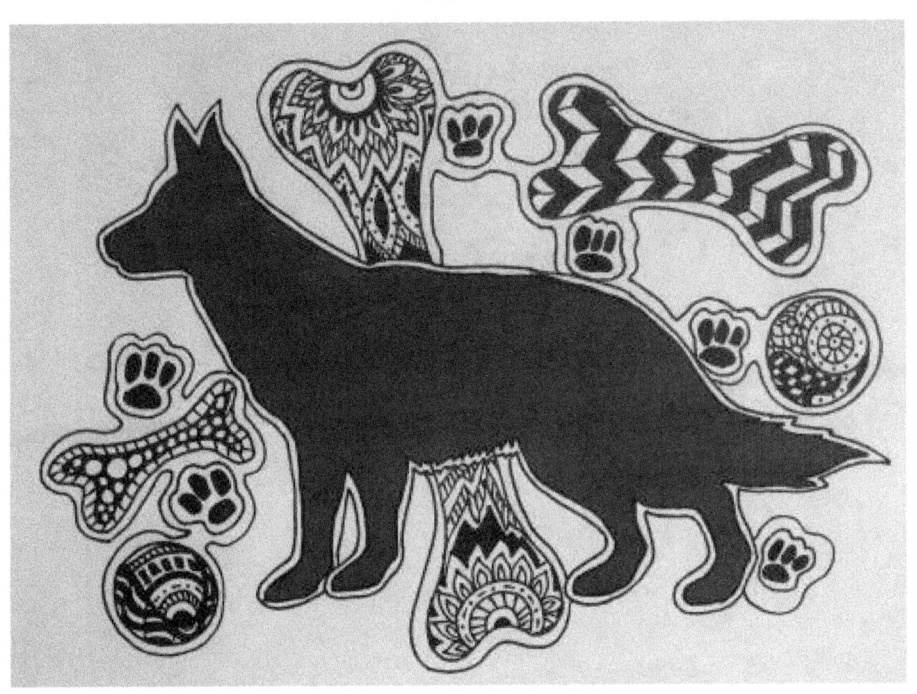

Step 6: Keep drawing the hide around ear, picture will direct you.

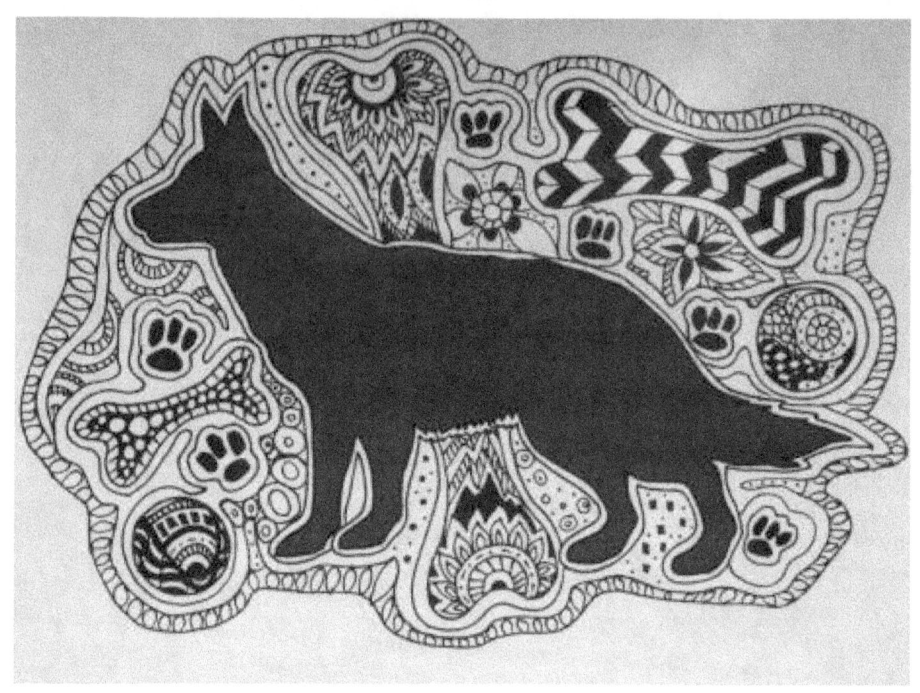

Step 7: Start attracting the hide point of interest close left eye, utilization picture to guide you.

Step 8: Keep filling in the hide on the left half of the face, picture will direct you.

Chapter 4 – How to draw image 4

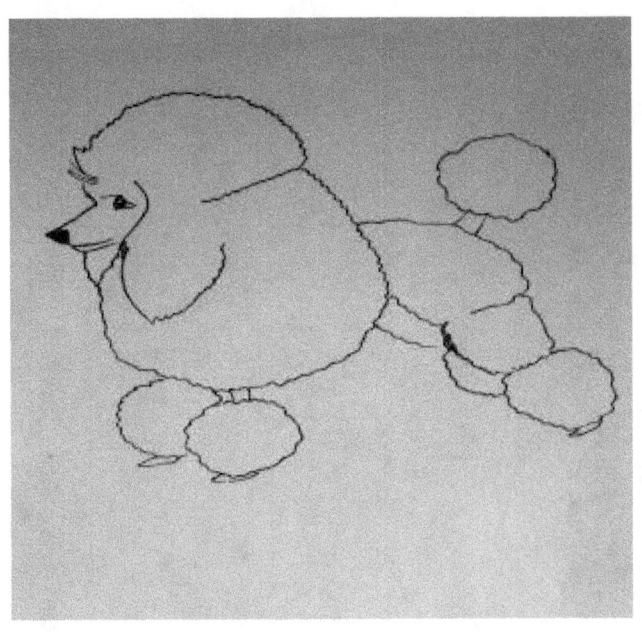

Step 1: Start with the head. It is a sideways snare shape with the shorter piece of the snare on the base. Make certain to add a little knock to the end of the long snare line. This is the nose. The top piece of the nose is twice the length of the base jaw.

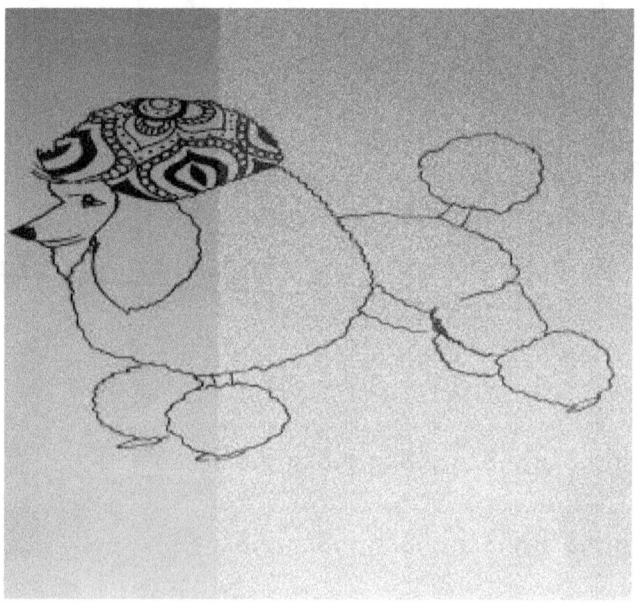

Step 2: Continue the top long nose line to make the bowed ear. Continue drawing the nose's base back and down to make the neck's front line.

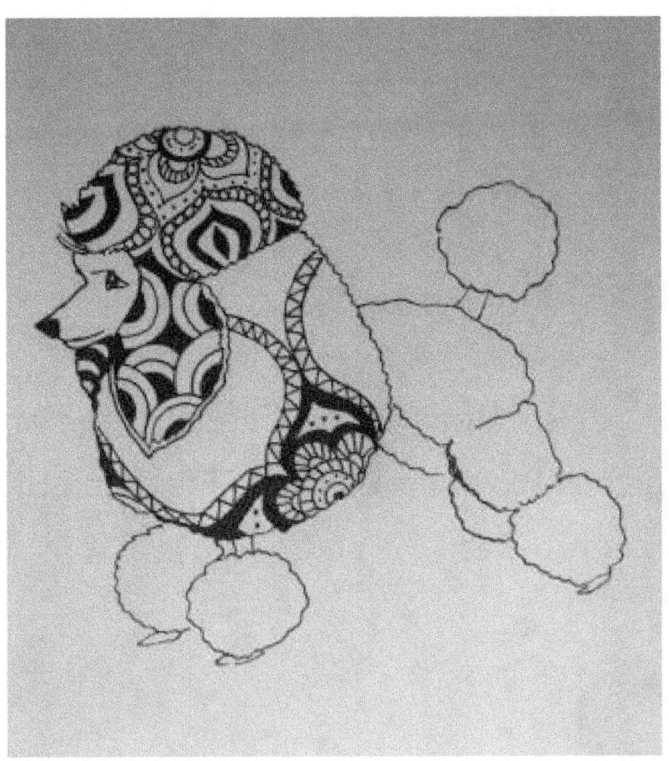

Step 3: Now draw a long line from the highest point of the head to make the back line. Bend the line down forcefully toward the end.

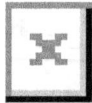

Step 4: Draw the rear end line down into the rear's back leg to the paw. Convey the line go down just about to the back line. Make the highest point of the back leg a touch more extensive than the base. Draw

the stomach line from the rear leg forward and include the front leg.

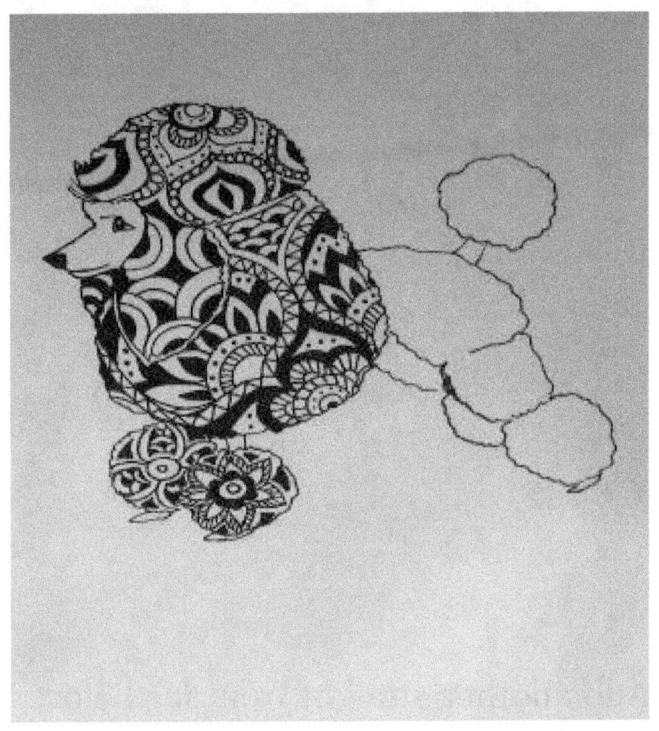

Step 5: The front leg line begins simply over the tummy line and proceeds down to the paw. It is the same size as the back leg. Draw the leg's front line go down to join the neck line.

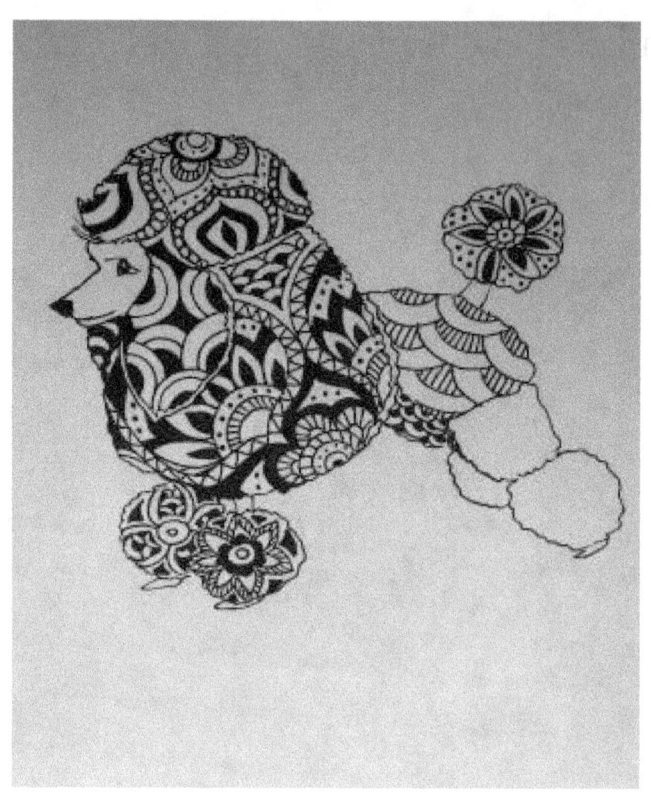

Step 6: Add another straight front leg before the first leg. Include another bended back leg before the first rear leg. At long last, from the back end draw a meager bended pointy tail.

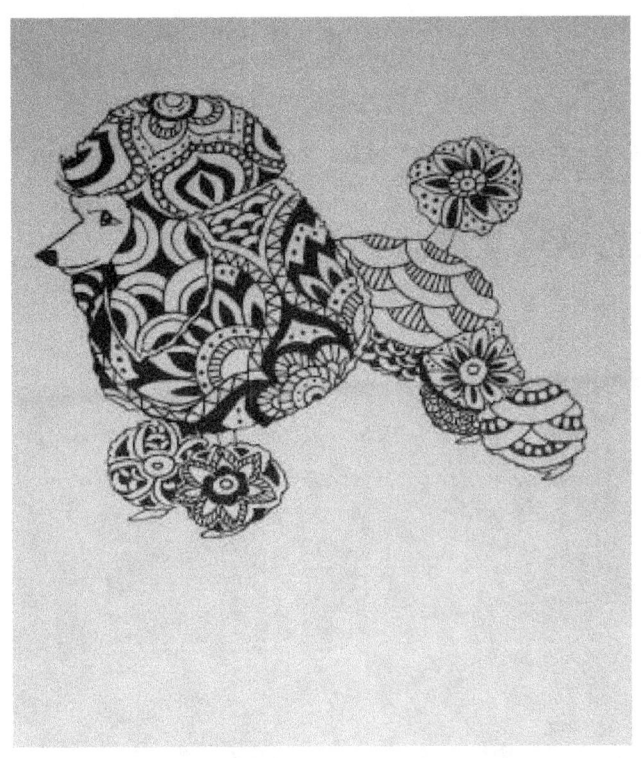

Step 7: Work on the shading part of the dog, so that the dog seems like a shaded one.

Chapter 5 – How to Draw Image 5

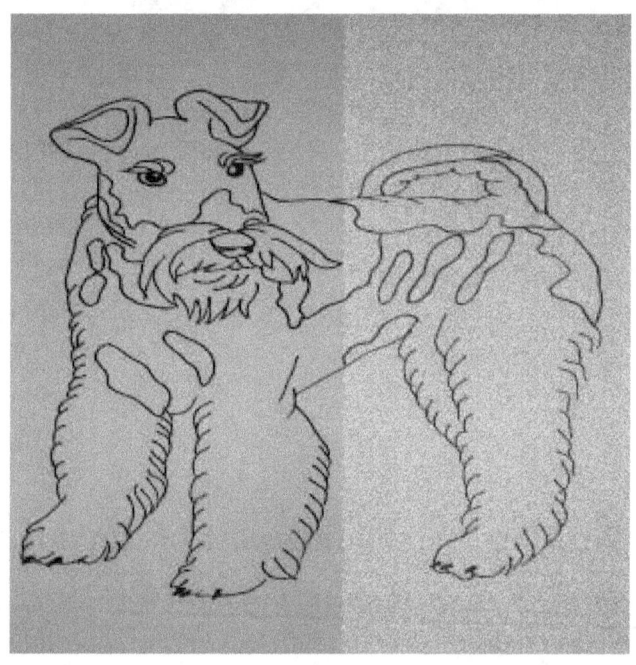

Step 1: In the first place draw the pooch's nose by drawing two bended lines.

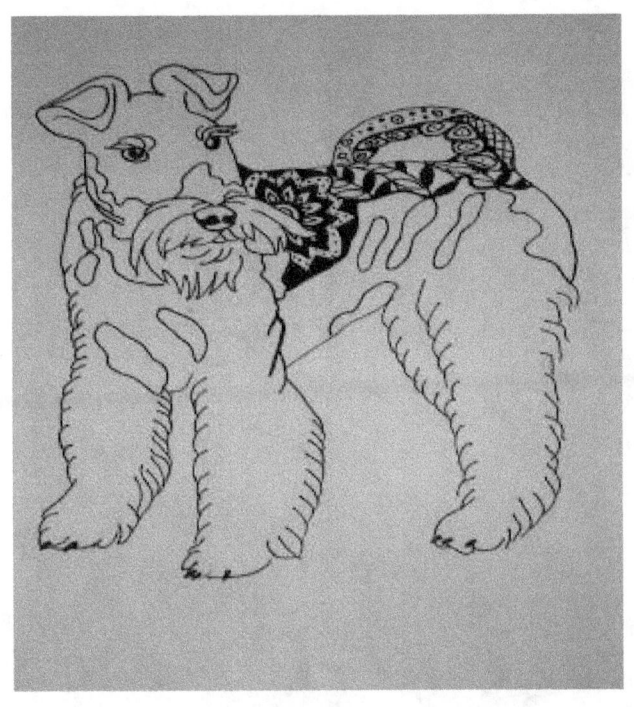

Step 2: Next draw the pooch's head utilizing a circle around his nose.

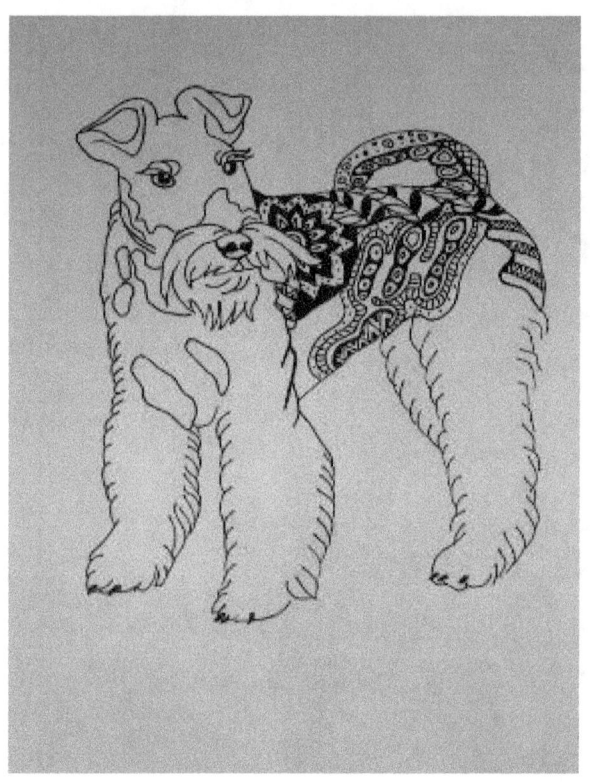

Step 3: Next draw the pooch's face. Include eyes nose and whatever is left of his mouth.

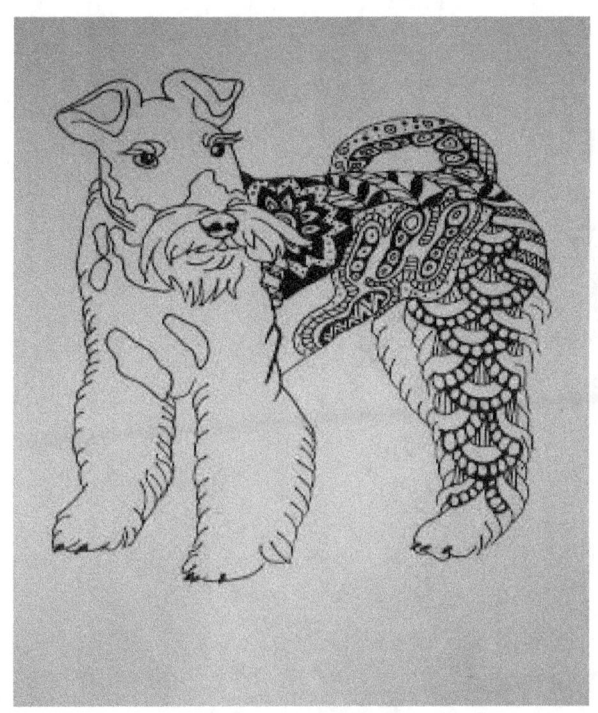

Step 4: Presently draw his two ears, and a tad bit of hide.

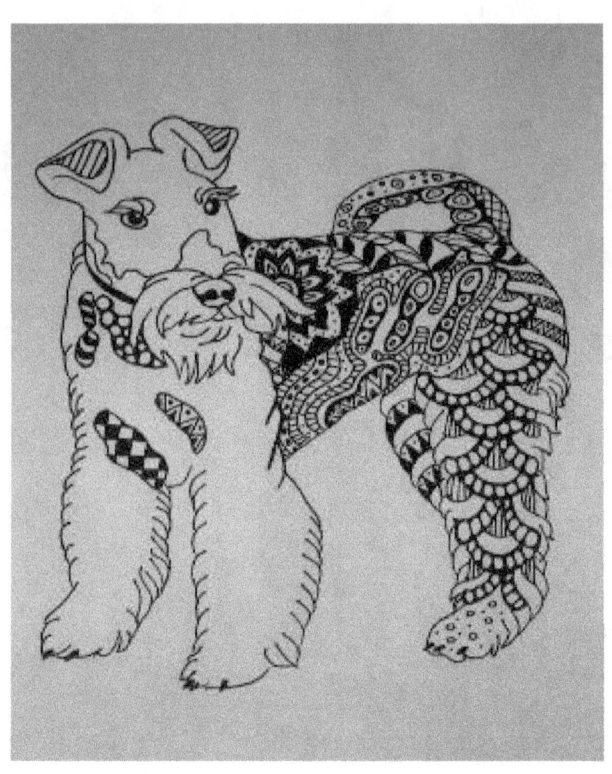

Step 5: Draw his two front feet and legs.

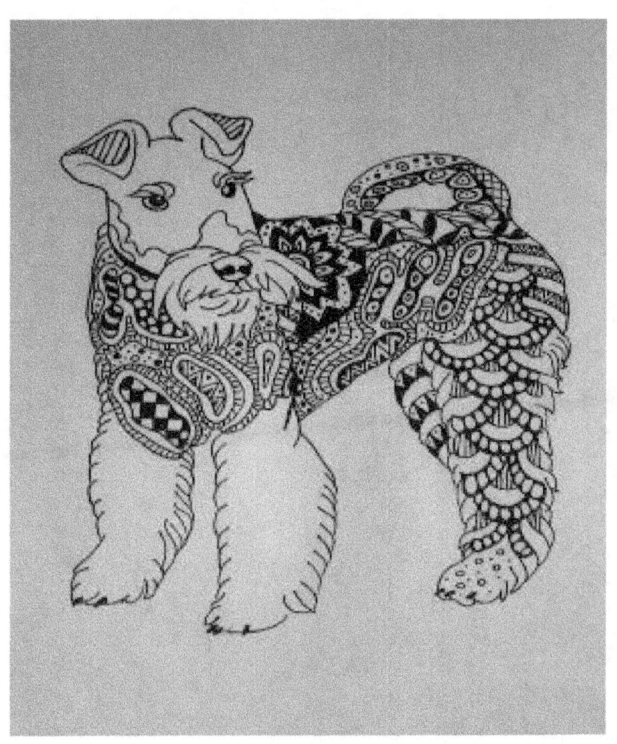

Step 6: Presently draw his stomach with a slanting line. Include the back of his legs, furthermore his back.

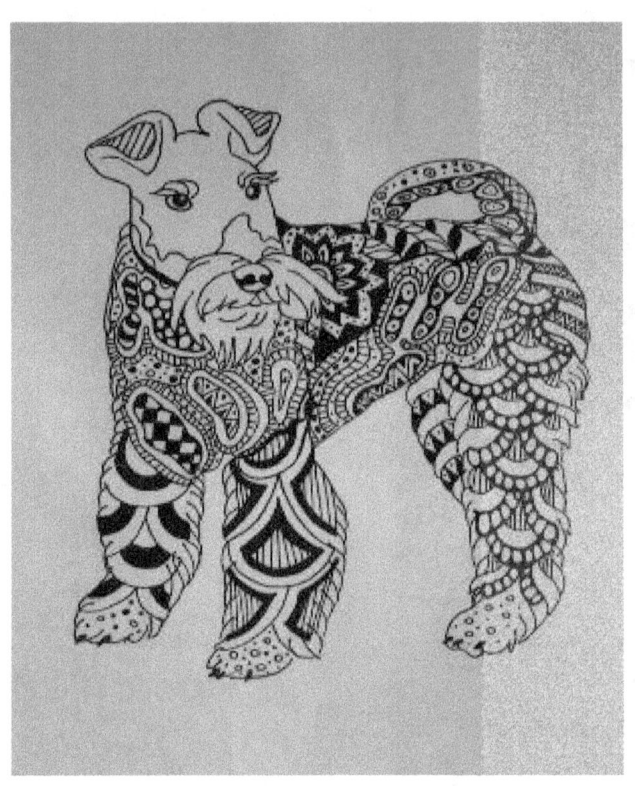

Step 7: Move a piece of his back leg.

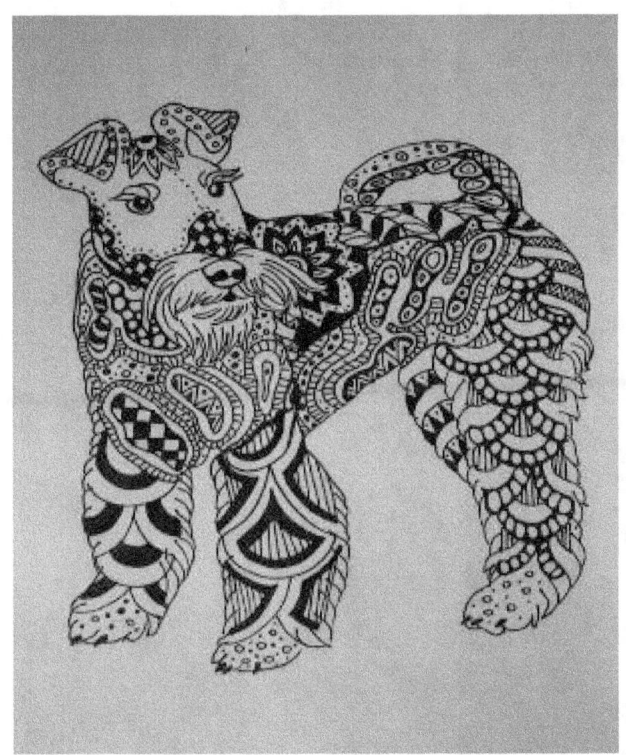

Step 8: With beautiful shading we have given the dog beautiful shading and thick as well in some parts.

Chapter 6: How to draw image 6

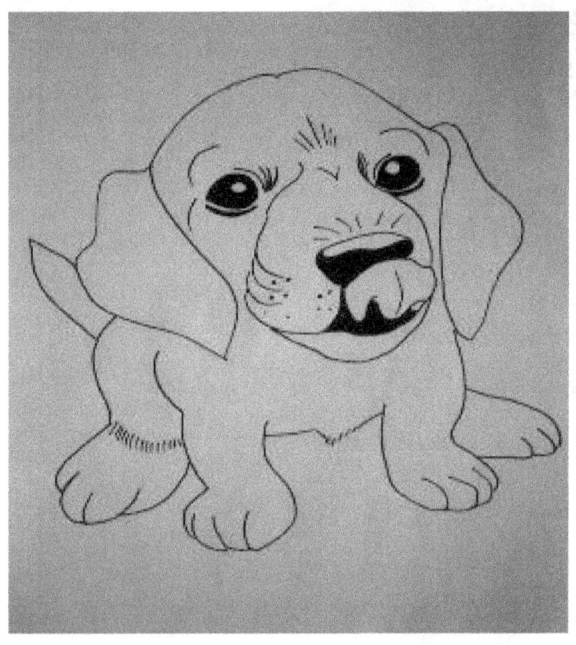

Step 1: Draw a major circle and two little covering circles at the base.

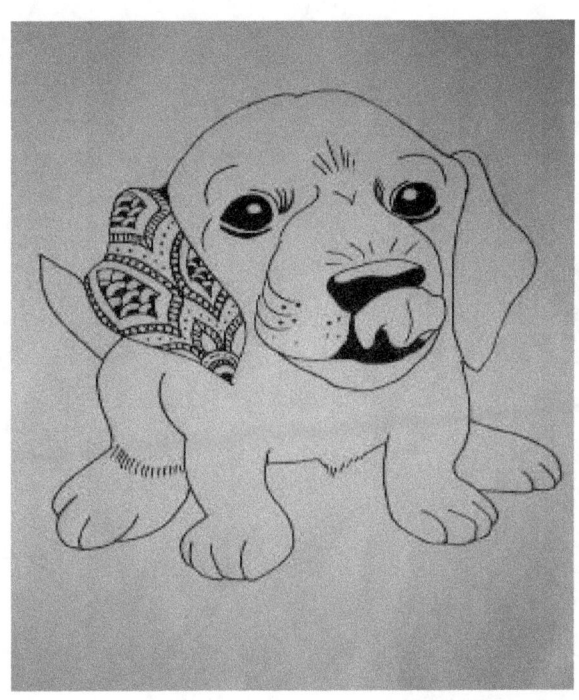

Step 2: Draw two inclined lines that is somewhat bended on the base appended to every little circle.

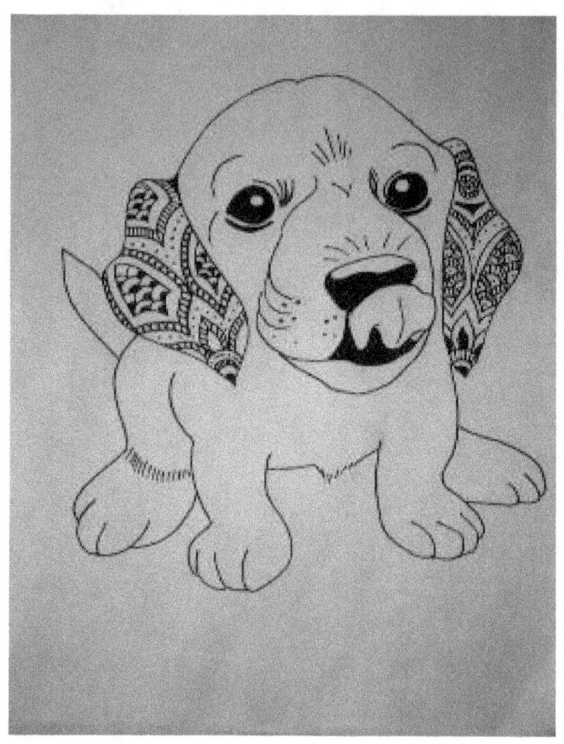

Step 3: Sketch a straight level line at the base and draw two half circles in front and another two behind.

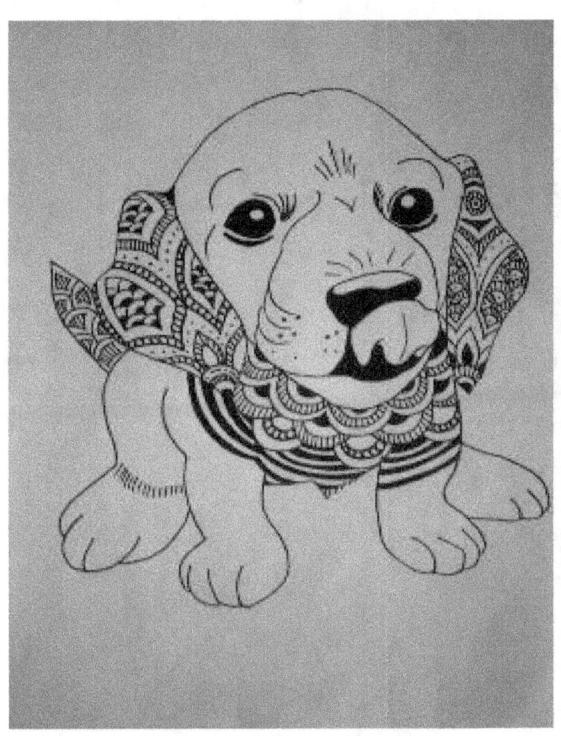

Step 4: Add another bended line at the back on every side. At the right side you can include a livened up tail.

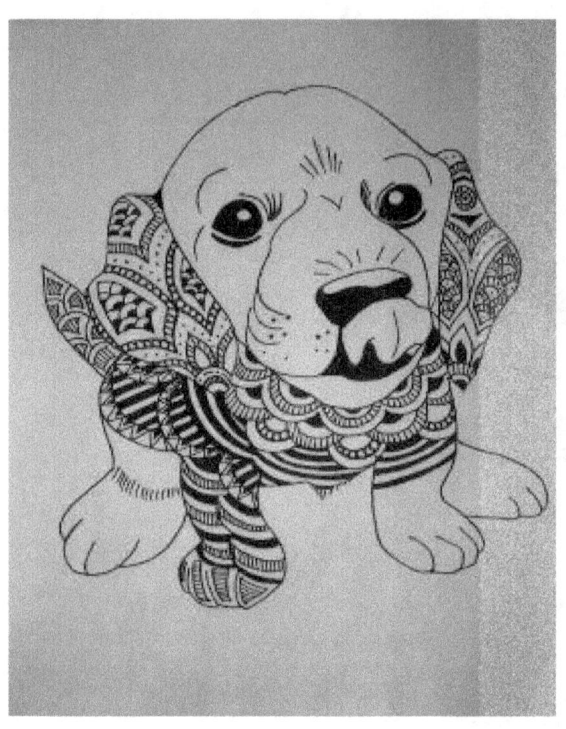

Step 5: Sketch the face by following the three's state circles. Include the ears pointed down every side.

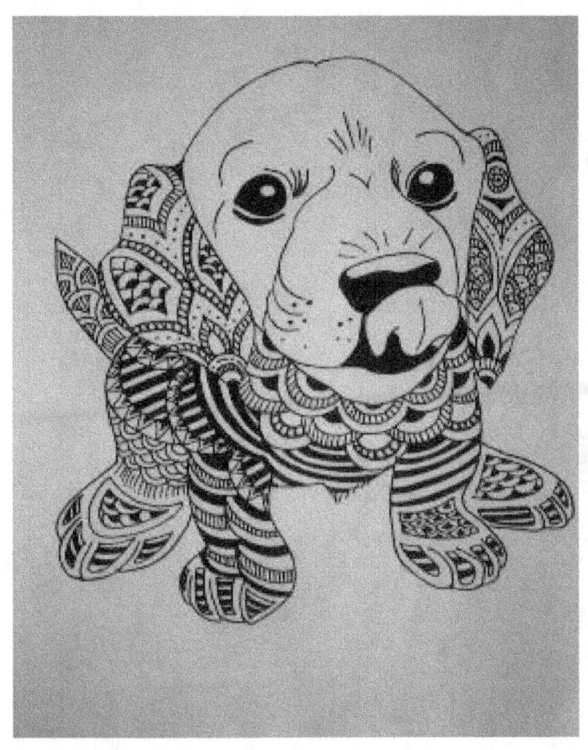

Step 6: Sketch the face utilizing two little circles for the eyes and two little bended lines for the temples and an elliptical for the nose.

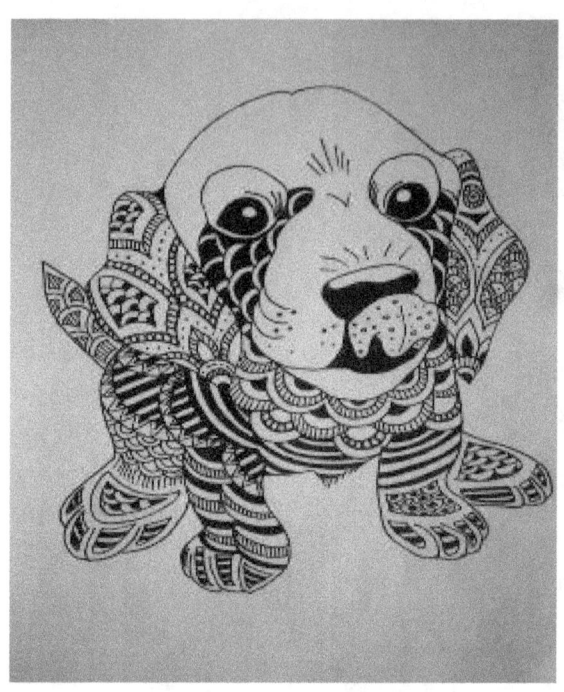

Step 7: Sketch the forelegs utilizing two parallel lines and another two parallel lines inside the half hover for the paws. You can include a neckline for outline.

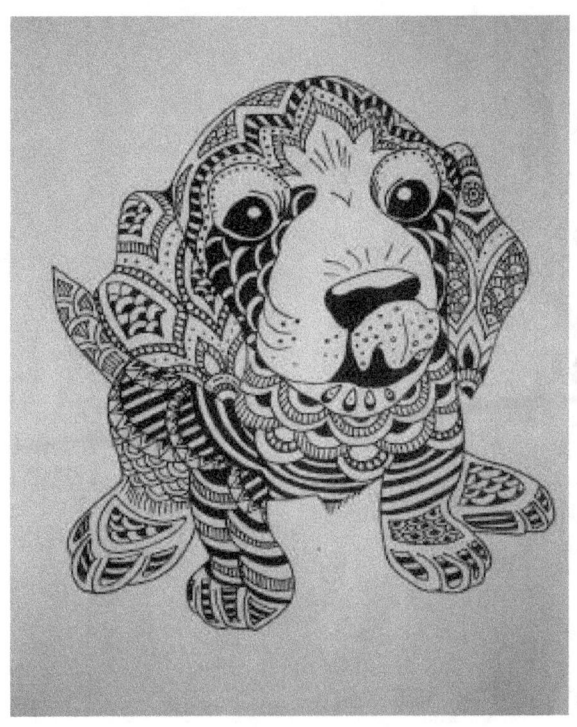

Step 8: You can draw the same little lines for the rear leg's paws.

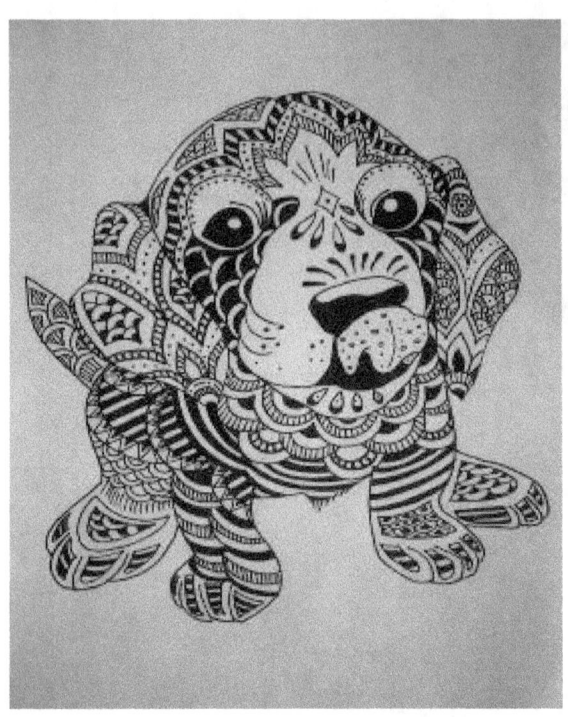

Step 9: Erase superfluous lines.

Step 10: Color or portrayal the drawing.

Conclusion

Intriguing Facts about Dogs

Numerous, numerous years back, individuals got to be companions with dark wolves – yes, wolves!

At the point when individuals initially found how shrewd wolves were, they started showing the wolves how to help them with their work.

They learned:

- Step by step instructions to force little wagons and trucks to assist individuals with moving things starting with one spot then onto the next.

- The most effective method to accumulate and keep sheep and bovines together into groups so they could be bolstered, drained or moved to somewhere else.

- The most effective method to "sniff out" feathered creatures and creatures for nourishment and caution individuals when there was risk adjacent.

- After some time, the considerable, awesome, extraordinary grandbabies of those agreeable wolves got to be what we know today as "dogs."

- Dogs of numerous types are adored by a great many individuals all over and are frequently called "man's closest companion" on the grounds that they are so benevolent, shrewd, supportive and exciting.

Did you know?

- A dog's nose has a print, much the same as human fingerprints that can be utilized to recognize them.

- A dog's feeling of smell is more than 100,000 times superior to anything a human's feeling of smell.

- A dog can hear something up to 820 feet away. That is more than 2 football fields!

- Most dogs have two layers of hide; an undercoat and an external coat.

- Dogs have almost 100 outward appearances, which incorporate the numerous courses in which they move, or hold their ears.

- The most prevalent names given to dogs are "Bear" for kid dogs and "Woman" for young lady dogs.

- A dog's wagging tail can flag what it is feeling. A high tail wagging in wide curves from side to side is a perky wag. A dog may be frightened if its tail is hanging low and scarcely wagging, or it is held between the legs. A high tail wagging rapidly may be a flag that the dog may assault.

- Dogs can likewise assist individuals with being more upbeat, sound and safe. They are prepared to work with police and fire fighters, to help individuals who are visually impaired move around, and are adoring allies to individuals who are debilitated or miserable.

- Much the same as kids, on the other hand, dogs need bunches of adoration, consideration and consideration to be the absolute best that they can be.

- There speak the truth 400 million dogs the world over.

- Dogs can have every distinctive sort of occupations, much the same as people. Some are police dogs who assist sniff with trip wrongdoing. A few dogs are called administration dogs, and they assist blind with peopling walk securely. Listening to dogs help their proprietors who are hard of hearing, and they can tell them when the telephone is ringing.

- Dogs are not really visually challenged.

- Dogs normally experience 14 years old.

- Dogs have a feeling of time. That is the reason your pooch knows when to welcome you consistently you get back home from school.

- Dogs rest for around 10 hours for every day.

- Much the same as human fingerprints, dogs can be distinguished by their nose prints.

- A larger number of dogs live in the United States than whatever other nation on the planet.

- A female dog is regularly pregnant for 63 days prior to she brings forth her litter of puppies.

- "Rough" and "Bailey" are two of the most prominent names of dogs.

- Dogs are the relatives of wolves. They were initially trained by people around 15,000 years prior.

- Dogs are more clung to people than whatever other creature, and that is the reason they are broadly known as "man's closest companion.

Whether you decide to paint pet dog representations or fuzzy feline works of art or perhaps put other wild creatures onto canvas, Artists are as particular and blended as these individuals come, conceivably not just in mastery (or scarcity in that department), all things considered outline and psyche set, yet a few things are shared, through situating our inventiveness in addition to objectives on to a bit of paper or canvas. The specific style of work of art is it can be procured at ages youthful and old. In the event that workmanship looks sublime to fairly a fledgling then that is most likely since they never invested any genuine effort representation or essentially outlining since leaving educating.

The whole procedure of seeing is by and large procured by numerous, and seeing is the imperative thing to painting and outlining, and drawing/portraying the essential thing to working with any routines. Attracting fundamentally adds up to measuring, guiding the brush to interpret a rendering seen with the eyes. The more flawless the extents, the more prominent like the theme that canvas will be similar to (yes, it might be much less difficult said than done!). The essential learning acknowledged precisely can lead a man toward ones goals.

Independent of whether you craving to paint another untamed life picture or speak to a scene loaded with uncommon fowls inside of a canvas, workmanship deer could in all likelihood be in the meantime agreeable notwithstanding peaceful. You might not need to be viewed as an astounding painter to paint wildfowl. Then again, you can undoubtedly hone it just like a charming art.

1. Start with a creatures' outline you need to paint. This is utilized as a part of the type of individual reference and that implies you will keep the attributes lessened. When you're bit of workmanship an area, sketch in the finishing also. You would potentially find it valuable to make utilization of photography to be an exploration thing or just to give a projection to help with proportions.

2. Paint the field above all else. Through acrylic paints, you'll have the capacity to consolidate typical water to debilitate the shading and blend hues. Moreover on the off chance that you ever want a tough foundation, an individual need to utilize a blend of two paints comparative in shading. This is the thing that offers your bit of workmanship a further expert visual advance and additionally incorporates state of mind to the thought. Certain perspectives require one to shut out the scenery relying upon your own outline.

3. Make coatings when men shade hair. You make hide that looks full and delicate by mixing the hide's shades and giving ones shading to dry out completely. Shade further coatings running the fields of lighter and also more profound dog's hide on every one layer. Utilize your brush to build up strokes in the dog's way hide.

4. Focus on the untamed life within the front of your specialty work. Creatures in your the foundation should contain less points of interest and will need to simply show the event of option animals. It is anything but difficult to use a wash created by including significantly more waters to ones paint to cover over essentially less important wild creatures as a simple approach to consolidate these into your background.

5. Give yourself time with the goal that you can give things a shot. Unquestionably, there are not really any specialists individuals who plan a radiant animal picture the first event these individuals attempt. Show tolerance and endeavor numerous courses to figure out what outline performs the best for your situation. You have the capacity to also think of dynamic untamed life and enjoy the procedure of bit of workmanship creatures from your own particular private selective depiction.

Assume you are given a task to paint a picture of your dog and you need to do this sans preparation with no info or related knowledge in workmanship or painting. This aide will assist you with beginning in making an astonishing dog representation that will be esteemed by numerous for quite a long while to come.

Before you start, it is vital to assemble the supplies that will make it feasible for you to effectively deliver the dog picture. These will incorporate a mixed bag of oil paints, bed blade, canvas, diverse brushes and a drawing pencil.

At the point when making a dog representation, the first step is to take a few photos of your dog in distinctive positions. Verify the photos are in shading. Lighting is the most critical component of an incredible dog representation. While taking the photos outside, verify the sun is before the dog to evade dull shadows crosswise over critical zones of your photos.

At the point when shooting the photos inside, try to keep up an unfaltering scope of light all through the space to avoid shadows. Try different things with different lighting conditions inside of the room you will utilize and change as important to counteract brilliant flares and impacts that may be undesirable in the subsequent representation. Endless supply of the pre-shoot, decide how and where your dog will posture. An easygoing representation is well worth taking into considering, as it tends to catch the quintessence of a dog's identity. Buy a representation outline that will supplement your finished dog picture.

When you have the ideal representation photos close by, you then make a fake up that will help you to envision the last painting. Focus the foundation that will be most suitable for your representation. The following step is to make a photos' representation and verifying that it is as exact as would be prudent.

Blend and match the different photos that you took amid your photograph shoot.

Make the first layer by covering the canvas in paint, while painting toward the hide. At this stage you ought not stress much over the exactness of shading. At the point when the first coat has dried out totally, apply a flimsy layer of liquin over the district you will be painting the hide.

Presently plunge the tip of your vast brush into the oil paint and start painting the first under-layer of surfaces and hide. At the point when the first under-layer has totally dried out, apply a flimsy layer of liquin over the work of art. The following step is to attempt and get the artistic creation to coordinate with the reference photo and displaying the hide of your dog. After the paint has dried, spread the entire canvas with a slender layer of liquin.

Presently go over the hide utilizing light hues to shape the hide further. Utilize a hues' blend you need to create the coveted shading for your dog. From that point, with the paint dried, again apply a dainty layer of liquin over the range.

Start to coat the darker hues over the highest point of the hide to thump back the light hues and include profundity and shadows. Invest more energy painting inside of fine detail and hide. Never forget to paint your hide from light to dim. Apply a light line of shading to mix in the root and tip.

Take a shot at the pet's declaration to verify it takes after that in the photo. This is the most critical of picture painting, as individuals are liable to take a gander at the expression more than whatever other piece of your dog representation.

The time has come to make the completing touches on your dog representation. Chip away at the eyes, around the ears, and the edges of your representation to create an awesome and eye getting completion. Let the picture dry out totally. At the point when all is done, tidy up and outline your dog picture in a fitting representation outlines.

Pet Portraits - how drawings and works of art of pets catch recollections that live for eternity

People and creatures have had a unique relationship for about 10,000 years since dogs were initially tamed. Creatures have gotten to be similar to individuals from the family, friends and family who we think about and who every have their own particular individual identity.

As we adore our pets to such an extent as consider them along these lines, it has turned out to be more regular for individuals to commission fine art to be done of their dog, feline, or other creature. The scope of styles being utilized has additionally expanded. Portrayals were before the most famous kind of picture, yet now individuals are swinging more to watercolor artistic creations, oil compositions, and even conceptual work of art (dynamic workmanship is a decent method for catching something uncommon about the identity of your pet that may not be communicated in a representation).

Watercolor works of art

Watercolor is an extraordinary method for getting a decent resemblance of your pet and of the view around them. It is especially great in the event that you need the representation of your pet to incorporate a spot they like to go, similar to their most loved field or the shoreline, on the grounds that watercolor artistic creations can truly make the scenes look wonderful.

Outlines

Representations are a decent method for truly catching the points of interest of your pet's face and individual components. This ordinarily functions admirably for close up representations and permits you to truly catch the individual identity, particularly in the eyes. Representations are generally delivered in high contrast yet can likewise look awesome in shading (consider this if, for instance, you have a ginger feline).

Oil Paintings

An oil painting is an incredible approach to get a picture of your pet in shading that can truly look dazzling and spotlight on the fundamental components of the individual creature. Oil painting is an exceptionally old and fantastic procedure that will frequently convey the most excellent results.

Dynamic Art

With dynamic workmanship you never recognize what's in store. The picture of your pet will to a great extent be down to the craftsman's impression, and in some cases the craftsman's temperament at the time the workmanship is made. Theoretical craftsmanship is not generally to everyone's taste but rather it can end up being a fabulous method for catching an one of a kind and intriguing understanding into the identity of your pet. This is not a typical decision of painting pets, but rather can some of the time create the most astonishing and intriguing results.